Table of Contents

Pupil Book Page		Accompaniment Book Page
9	The One String Balance	1
10	L-o-n-g Notes: Row, Row, Row Your Boat	2
11	The 'D' Song	3
12	Running 'D's	4
13	Another 'D' Song: Hot Cross Buns	5
15	Walking 'E's: Mary Had a Little Lamb	6
15	Long 'E's: London Bridge	6
16	Mixed up 'D's and 'E's	7
17	The 'D' - 'E' March	8
18	Walking 'G's: Yankee Doodle	9
19	Hot Cross 'G's	9
20	The Fingers Song	10
21	Skips	10
22	G-D Plonks; A Tune to Play	11
24	Mr Sun	12
25	Where's the Mouse	12
28	The Real Hot Cross Buns	13
29	Circles	14
30	Fingers in a Row	14
31	The Duke of York	15
32	Walking 'A's: Au Clair de la Lune	16
33	Bow Tricks: String Changing	16
34	Up and Down	17
35	Mary Had a Little Lamb	18
36	Lightly Row	19
36	Lightly Row: Trio Arrangement	20
36	Lightly Row: Trio Parts	22
37	Finger Tricks: String Hopping	24
37	Hot Cross Finger Tricks	24
38	London Bridge	24
39	Twinkle, Twinkle Little Star	25

Pupil Book Page		Accompaniment Book Page
39	Twinkle: 2nd or Harmony Part	26
40, 41	Rhythmic Variations on the Tune of 'Twinkle'	27
42	Old MacDonald Had a Farm	28
43	This Old Man	29
44	Finger Tricks: Skipping	29
45	Finger Tricks: Doubles; Hot Pepper	29
46	Shepherds' Hey	30
47	D Major Scale	30
48	Finger Tricks: Crab Walking	31
49	Short'nin' Bread	31
50	Time Signatures: Four in the Bar	32
51	Three in the Bar	32
51	Two in the Bar	33
52	French Folk Song	34
52	French Folk Song: 2nd or Harmony Part	36
53	Kookaburra	38
53	Kookaburra: 2nd or Harmony Part	39
56	Frere Jacques	40
57	Row, Row, Row Your Boat	41
58	I'm a Peanut	42
58	I'm a Peanut: Trio Parts	43
59	Crazy	44
60	Jingle Bells	45
60	Jingle Bells: Trio Parts	46
61	Joy to the World	48
61	Joy to the World: Quartet Parts	50
62	Can-Can	52
62	Can-Can: Pizzicato Bass Part	53
63	German Folk Dance	54
63	German Folk Dance: Quartet Parts	55

The number in the top corner preceded by ♪ is the page number in the pupil's book.

Tricks to Tunes

Introduction

This set of tutors has been developed from my own teaching needs as a string teacher in schools for many years. It has been designed for the systematic instruction of mixed string instruments in groups.

The tutor is aimed at the primary age group, but the approach is also suitable for older beginners.

The title of the tutor suggests the teaching method followed. Reliance is placed on 'tricks' for the children's fingers or bows, which are fun and stimulating when done in a group. At the same time reading skills are developed. Each page represents a small progression in both musical and technical development. It is often the case that children who learn to play by finger numbers have difficulty in making the transition to proper notation. With this method, reading is encouraged from the very first lessons.

The order of progress is from a single open string stepwise to the scale of 'D' Major. One divergence from the usual approach is that the note 'G' is taught after 'E' but before 'F#', which better develops the left hand position, especially for cellists. The tunes in this section of the tutor are based on the minor 3rd interval and correlate with the Kodaly method in classroom music. As the primary intention of this tutor is for group tuition of mixed string instruments, the note 'A' is presented as an open string (except for the double bass). It is left to the discretion of the teacher to decide at what point to introduce the use of the fourth finger to violin and viola pupils.

A theory homework section is included at the end of most learning segments.

Book I is intended to cover the first year of group tuition, based on a school year of forty weeks. This will, of course, vary according to the age of the children, the size of the group and the extent of previous musical experience.

The additional repertoire section at the end of the book is included as:
- extension work for pupils who reach the end of the book before the rest of the group,
- additional work for those who want it, or
- end of year concert pieces.

As far as possible all of the tutors are identical in content. The only variations in the violin, viola and cello books are clefs and fingers. However, due to the tuning of the double bass, this tutor is slightly different in a few places. The actual notes being played on the bass are the same with the exception of Bow Tricks: Trickier String Changing on page 33 and Finger Tricks: String Hopping on page 37.

Most importantly, this set of tutors is designed to make playing music fun, as it should be!

Audrey Akerman

How the Accompaniment Book Works

The accompaniments have been kept simple so that parents or siblings, with limited music skills or piano-playing abilities, can play along with the pupil. Also, some of the tunes, such as 'Lightly Row' on page 36, have been arranged for duets or trios so that the slightly more advanced pupils can play along with the beginners. This is to provide supplementary teacher resources for use at school assemblies and concerts. Individual parts have been printed in this book to allow the teacher to provide single copy parts as needed for a class group.

The accompaniments for many of the simple pieces at the beginning of the book are arranged so that the right hand piano part is suitable as a violin accompaniment for the teacher to play.

Most of the accompaniments for the single note 'tricks' and tunes at the beginning of the pupil's book appear later in their book as solo pieces for them to play.

All of the pupil's parts written above the piano accompaniments are in treble clef. They are, of course, in the relevant clef for each instrument in the individual tutors.

The pages in the pupil's book are shown in the top corner of each page preceded by ♪ and listed in the index for easy reference.

Advice to Parents

Learning to play a stringed instrument is a long slow process. The skills required to play well are developed gradually through constant repetition. The purpose of this tutor is to try to make practice more fun by appealing to a child's natural desire to do 'tricks'. Try to encourage your child to play the 'tricks' by feel, not looking at their fingers. The ultimate aim is to play them with their eyes shut.

If you are a piano-playing parent, use this book to accompany your child during practice sessions. This will help to develop a better sense of pitch and a feel for beat and rhythm. It will also make practice a lot more fun. If you can not play the piano, consider having lessons and learning along with your child.

Practice sessions should be little and often. Ten minutes twice a day is far more valuable than an hour twice a week. Make it part of the daily routine.

Follow the Mouse

Learning to read notes is rather like following the movement of a mouse as it runs up and down on a five-rung ladder.

Cut out, copy or trace the mouse from this page
and use it to represent a note
on the opposite page.

Challenge the pupils
to follow the
mouse.

At this stage the pupil's book has neither time nor key signatures.
The tune 'Kookaburra' comes later in the pupil's book on page 53.

The One-String Balance: Kookaburra

♪ **10**

To play long notes, encourage the pupil to use long bow strokes with a relaxed arm 'opening and closing' from the elbow.
The pupil's part is written in Common Time without a time signature.
The tune 'Row, Row, Row Your Boat' comes later in the pupil's book on page 57.

L-o-n-g Notes: Row, Row, Row Your Boat

It is not necessary at this stage to introduce complicated subdivisions of the bow. However, the pupil should develop a feeling of short bow for short note and long bow for long note.

The 'D' Song

♪ 12

Short, quick notes can be difficult for the beginner. Try to encourage a relaxed bowing arm without raising the shoulder.

Running 'D's

Repeat as necessary for practice.

'Hot Cross Buns' is a simple melody familiar to all children. It is used here to help develop a sense of rhythm and an understanding of the rhythmic values of the different kinds of notes.

Another 'D' Song: Hot Cross Buns

♪ 15 **Walking 'E's: Mary Had a Little Lamb**

Long 'E's: London Bridge

♪ 16

The pupil should be helped to understand the relationship between the movement of the note on the stave and the finger on the fingerboard. They need to observe the note stepping up or down and to follow this movement with their finger.
Encourage the pupil to listen carefully to get the note 'E' in tune.

Mixed up 'D's and 'E's

♪ 17

Young pupils need to develop a strong sense of rhythm as well as pitch. Counting the beats in groups of four could be emphasised in this piece.

Suggested activity: Divide the class into groups. Each group can then take turns playing the tune, playing a percussion instrument, clapping the beat or marching in time to the music. In this way the tune can be repeated many times without the lesson becoming boring.

The 'D'-'E' March

Walking 'G's: Yankee

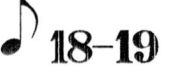

Hot Cross

♪ 20-21

The Fingers Song

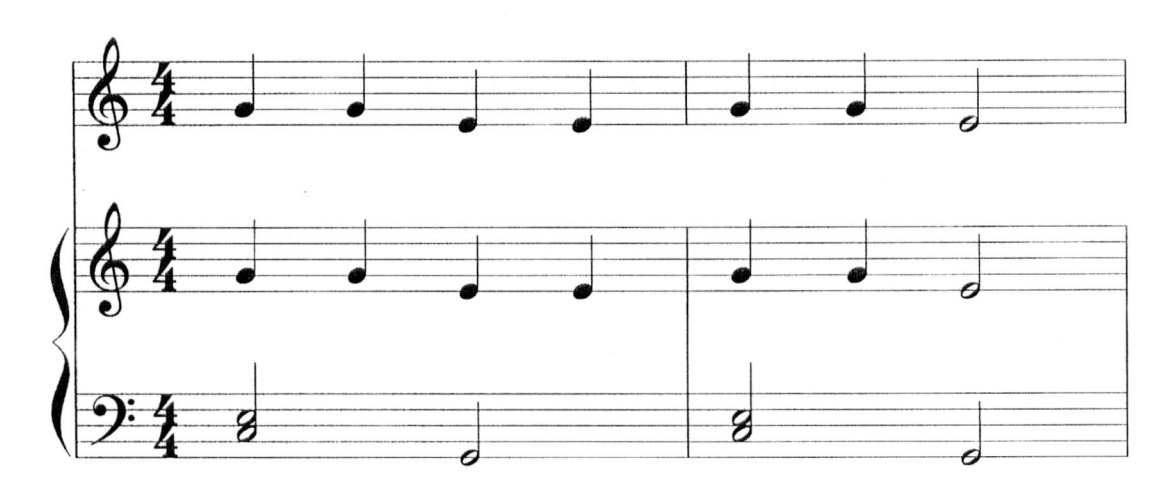

Skips

10

G-D Plonks

♪ 22

This is an exercise or 'trick' to help develop -
1. The correct placement of the hand and fingers to get the note 'G' in tune.
2. The co-ordination of the left hand fingers with the right hand bowing arm.

A Tune to Play

Mr Sun

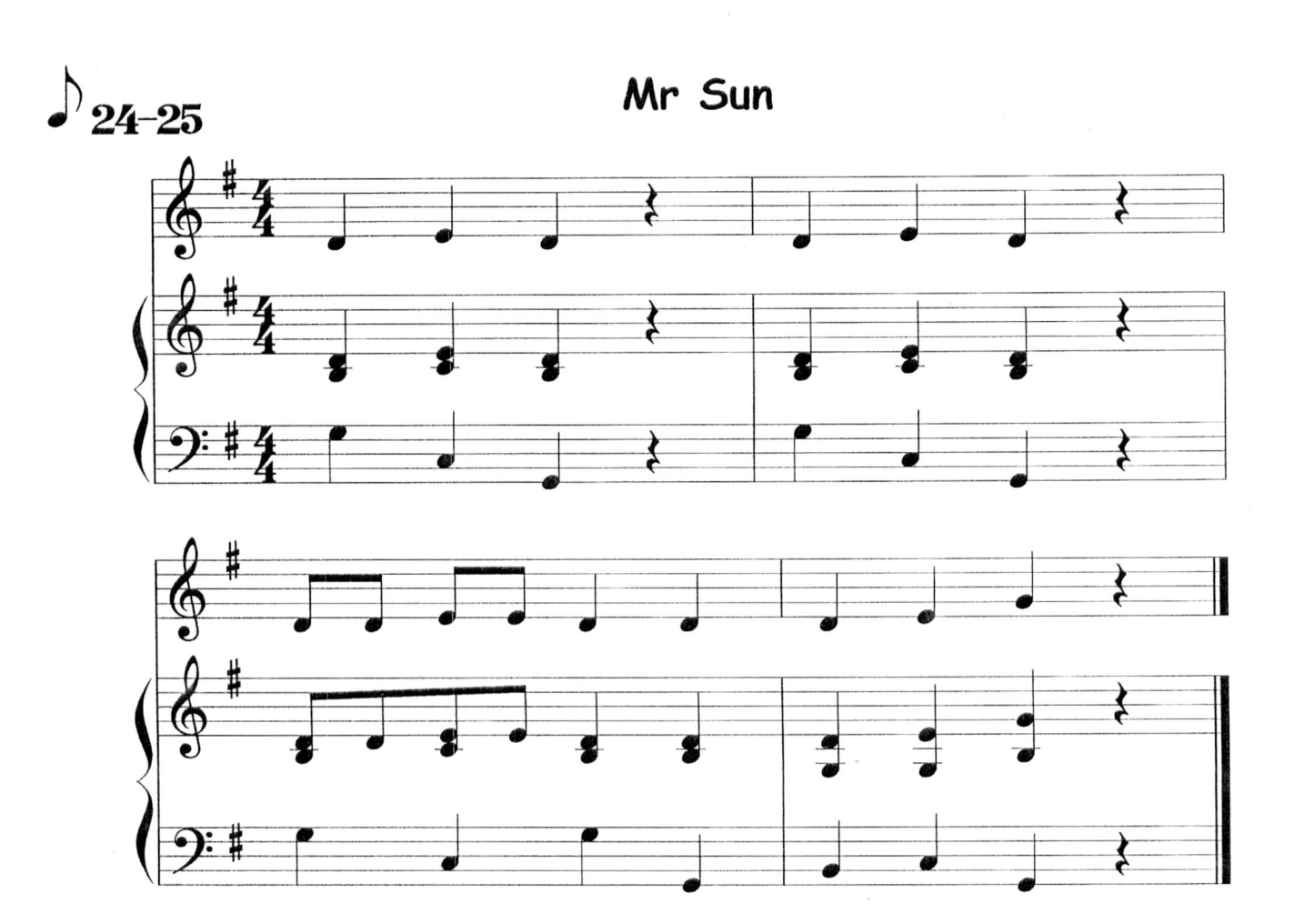

Where's the Mouse?

'F sharp' is a black note on the piano and is higher than a natural 'F'. The pupils, especially violin and viola players, may need to be reminded that 'F sharp' lives just behind 'G'. The finger must be placed correctly to get this note in tune.

The Real Hot Cross Buns

Circles

Fingers in a Row

♪ 31

Like all the pieces of music so far in this tutor, 'The Duke of York' is written in 4/4 time. However, it starts on the fourth beat of the bar. The teacher should explain the use of the anacrusis according to the development level of their own class.

The Duke of York

♪ 32-33

Walking 'A's: Au Clair de la Lune

Bow Tricks: String Changing

Note: On page 33 of the tutor the double bass notes are different from the other instruments in 'Bow Tricks: Trickier String Changing'.

The primary aim of this tutor is for the group tuition of mixed string instruments. For this reason the note 'A' has been presented in the pupil's book only as the next open string. However, it is an opportune time for the teacher to introduce the use of the fourth finger to the violin and viola students. Children will enjoy the skill of being able to play one note in two ways. The pupils can then choose (with teacher's guidance!) when to use the open string and when it is best to use the fourth finger. It is recommended though, that the fourth finger be taught before reaching 'Finger Tricks: Skipping' on page 44 in the pupil's book.

Up and Down

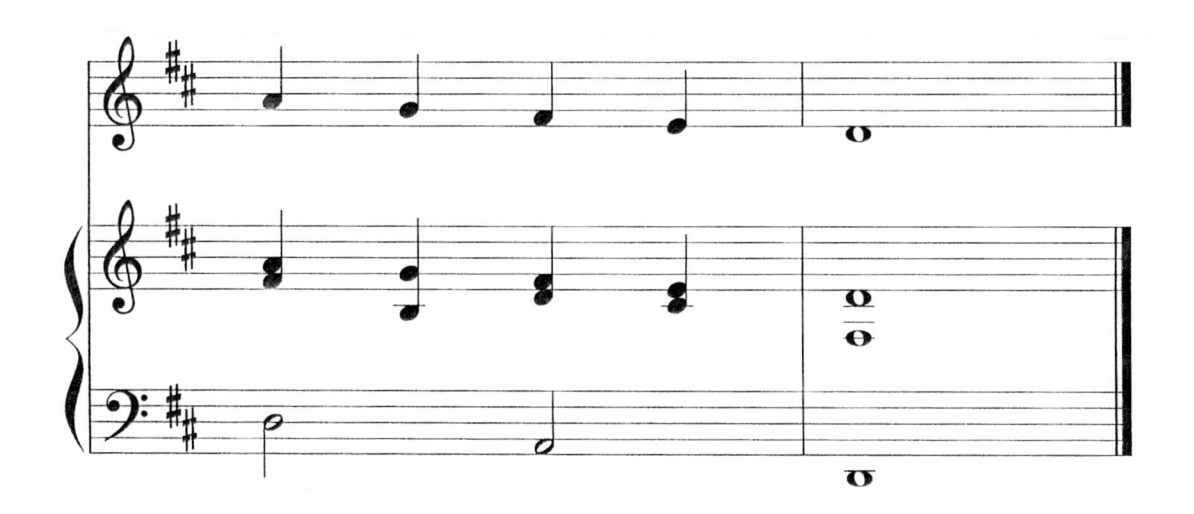

Mary Had a Little Lamb

This accompaniment of 'Lightly Row' has been arranged as a trio on the following pages. In this version it can be used as a school assembly or concert item, the beginners playing the 1st part or melody with the more advanced pupils playing the harmony parts.

♪ 36

Lightly Row

Lightly Row: Trio Arrangement

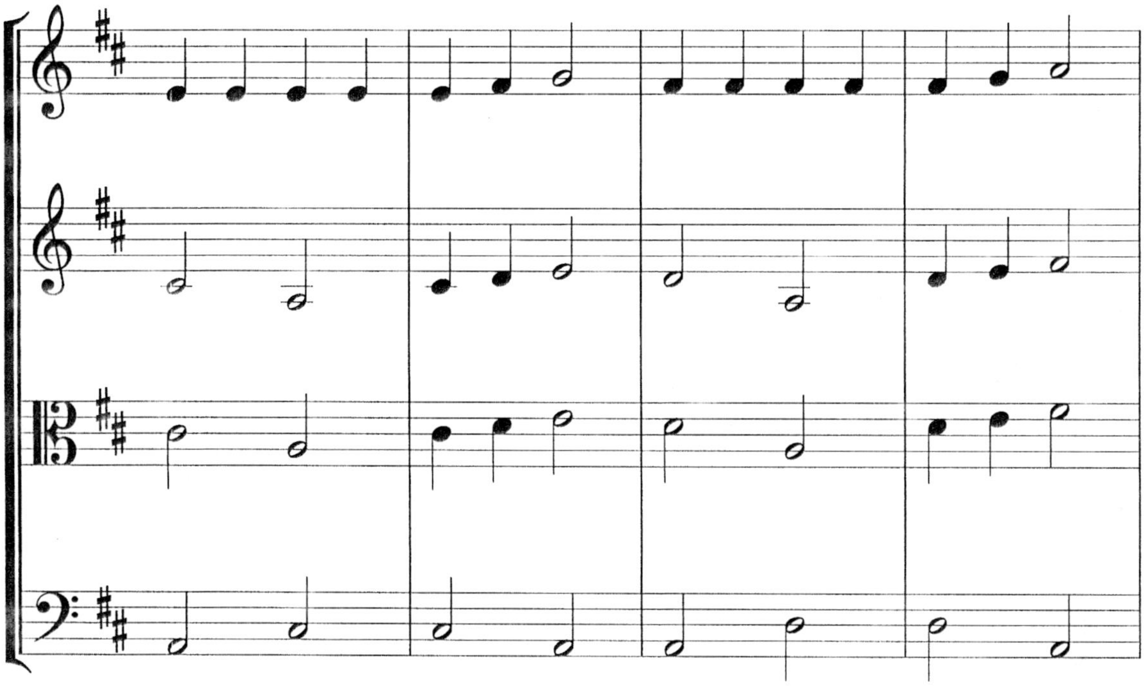

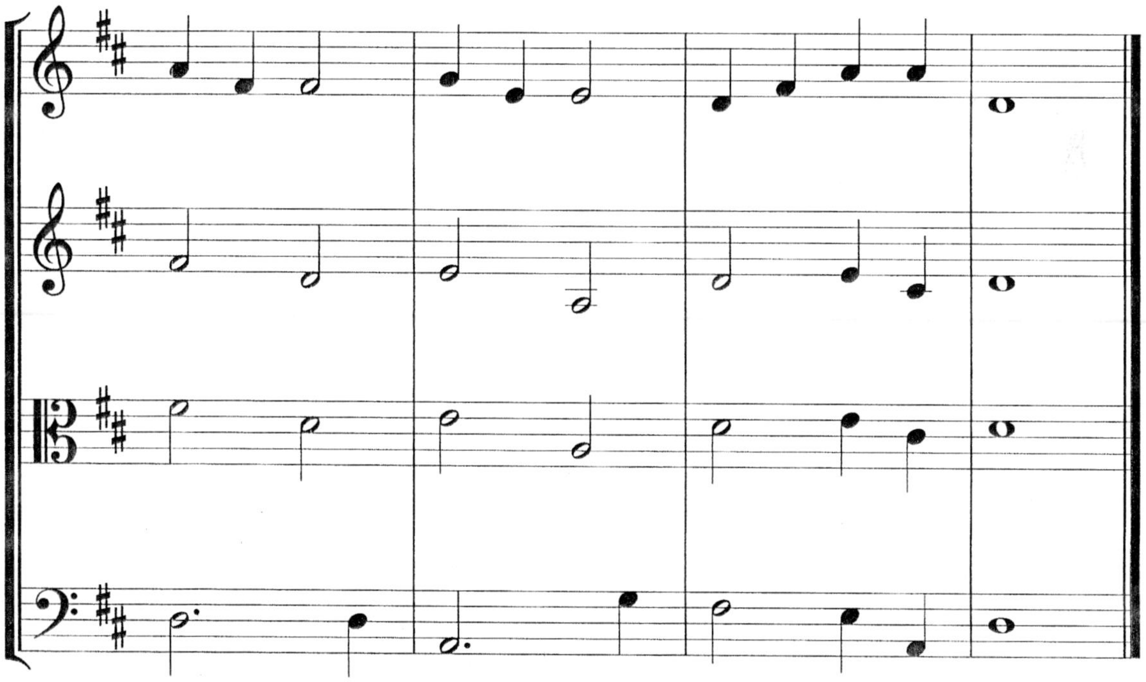

Lightly Row: Trio Parts

Lightly Row: Trio Part

♪ 37-38

Finger Tricks: String Hopping
The notes used for this trick in the double bass tutor are different from the other parts due to the different tuning of the bass strings.

Hot Cross Finger Tricks
The accompaniment is the same as 'Another 'D' Song' on page 13.

London Bridge

Twinkle, Twinkle Little Star

♪ 39   **Twinkle: 2nd or Harmony Part**

Rhythmic Variations on the Tune of 'Twinkle'

The concept of counting the beat, particularly fractional beats, is an abstract one which many children find difficult to understand at first.

However, a sense of rhythm in music is a natural feeling which can be developed through repetition and experience.

The well-known tune of 'Twinkle' lends itself perfectly as a theme for simple rhythmic variations.

These variations are also a 'fun way' to develop a natural feeling for bow control, bow distribution, bow retakes and so on.

Pupils should have memorised the tune before attempting the variations.

Some of the rhythms use note values which have not yet been introduced in the tutor, so it is suggested that each variation is taught by memory using the rhythmic structure of the words. For example, number 6 is 'one kookaburra' per crotchet beat.

The variations can be used as simple studies, the pupil learning the rhythms one by one while continuing to work through the tutor.

♪ 42

Check that the pupils understand : means to repeat.
This tune is based on the movement of the fingers
as in the 'G-D' Plonks trick on page 22.
Make sure that the 'G' finger stays in tune.

Old MacDonald Had a Farm

This Old Man

♪ 43-44-45

Finger Tricks: Skipping

The same accompaniment can be used for 'Doubles' and 'Hot Pepper'.

♪ 46-47

Key signatures are introduced in the pupil's book on this page.

Shepherds' Hey

D Major Scale

Finger Tricks: Crab Walking

♪ 48-49

Short'nin' Bread

♪ 50–51

Time Signatures

Four in the Bar

Three in the Bar

Two in the Bar

♪ 52

A second part is included in this arrangement so that more advanced pupils can play along with the beginners.

French Folk Song

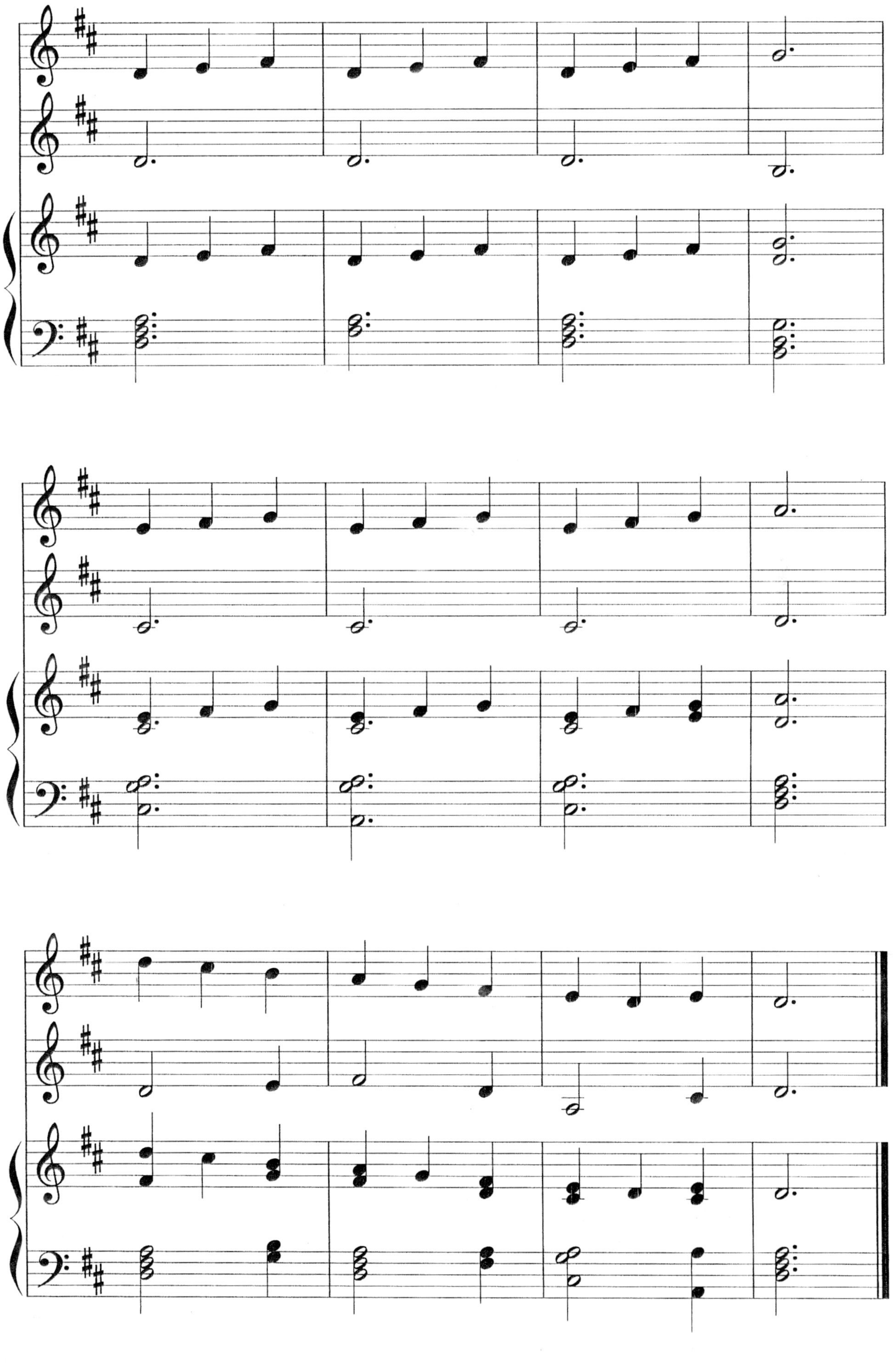

French Folk Song: 2nd or Harmony Part

♪ 52

♪ 53

This tune can be played by a class group as a round as well as in parts.

Kookaburra

Kookaburra: 2nd or Harmony Part

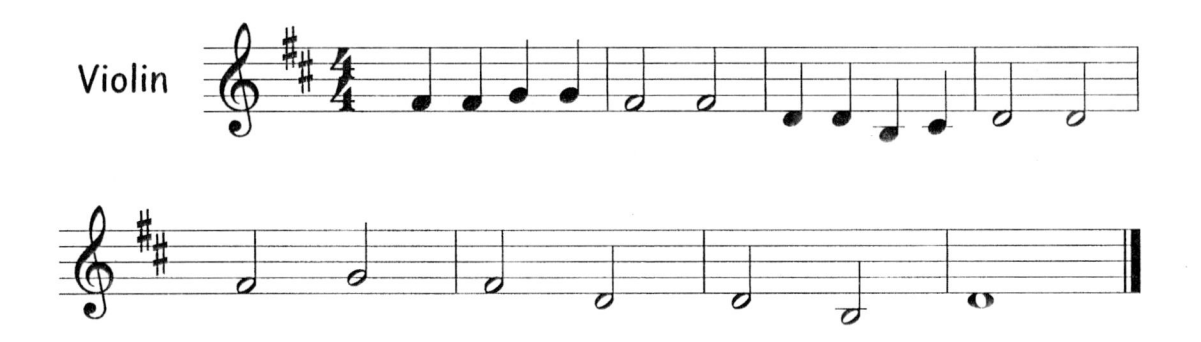

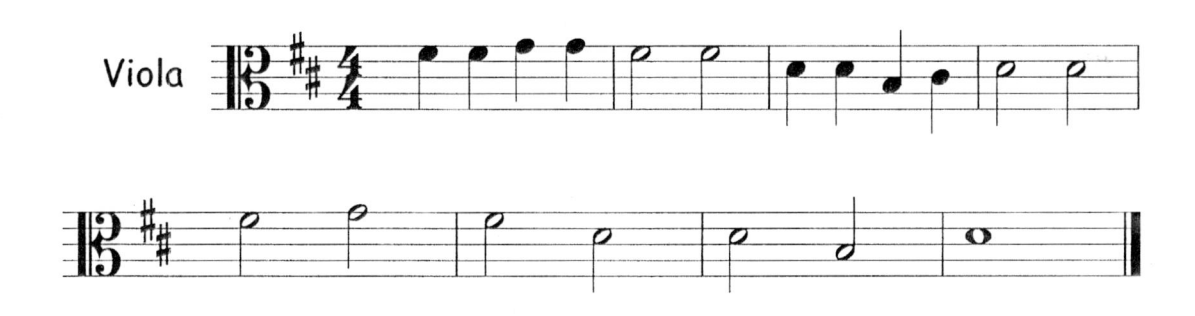

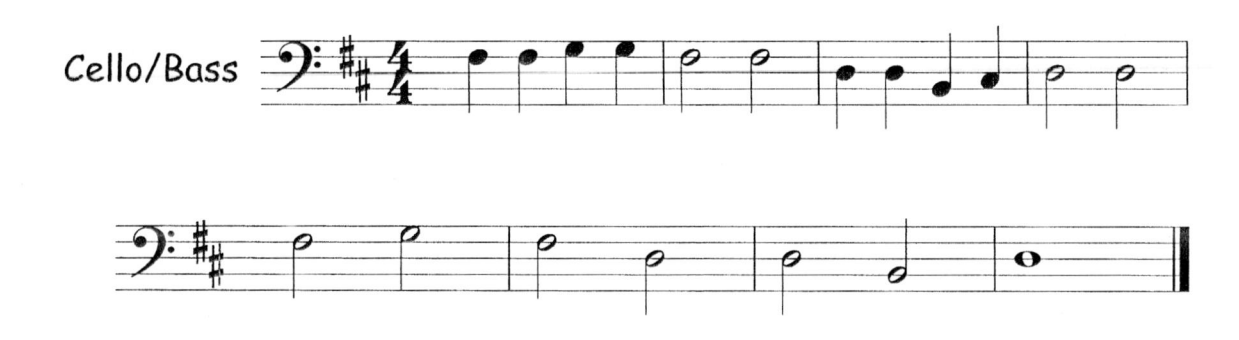

Frere Jacques

Row, Row, Row Your Boat

I'm a Peanut

I'm a Peanut: Trio Parts

Crazy

The left hand piano part is also suitable as a cello part for a duet.

Cello part

Jingle Bells

Jingle Bells: Trio Parts

♪ 60

Cello/Bass
(3rd part)

♪61

Joy to the World

49

Joy to the World: Quartet Parts

Violin II

Violin III
(Viola: Treble Clef)

50

61

Can-Can

Offenbach 1819-1880

♪ 62

The left hand part of the piano accompaniment is suitable for the cello or bass to play as a second part with the violins and violas.

Can-Can: Pizzicato Bass Part

German Folk Dance

German Folk Dance: Quartet Parts

German Folk Dance: Quartet Parts